OPTIMISE

OPTIMISE

5 SIMPLE STEPS TO ELEVATE YOUR TEAM'S CAPACITY USING ASANA

JANE ANDERSON

The perfect guide for World Class Thought
Leaders, Speakers and Consultants

ꓸꓸ asana

Editing: Kristen Lowrey

Typeset by BookPOD

ISBN: 978-0-6485022-4-1 (pbk)
eISBN: 978-0-6485022-5-8 (ebook)

A catalogue record for this book is available from the National Library of Australia

NATIONAL LIBRARY OF AUSTRALIA

Contents

Introduction

As a consultant myself, I face many of the same unique challenges that you do. It can be difficult to both deliver my services to my clients and run my business. It can be challenging to keep open lines of communication with my team when I'm travelling for speaking gigs or workshops. It can be tricky to keep visibility with work and task completion with a widespread team and all my other commitments.

For a long time, I struggled with these challenges. I knew that having the proper project management system could bring a huge amount of clarity and stress relief. But I struggled to find the right one. In fact, since beginning my practice, I've been through five different project management systems. And until I found Asana, I was really just going from one nightmare to another even bigger nightmare. Over the years I moved from Solve360 to Trello to Pipedrive to Insightly. Each time I felt like I was getting closer, but nothing was ever good enough.

At the time, I was also trying to understand why projects within my practice were floundering. I couldn't understand what was happening within my own business. All the insights were hidden, and I was lost. I had to keep asking my team what was going on, which meant that I began to lose trust in their capabilities.

Coming from a corporate background, I knew that I needed something like Microsoft but designed for my smaller consulting practice. Something that could embrace all the projects I had, from client delivery to keynotes. And then I found Asana.

Once I set up Asana, it captured everything that was happening in my practice and with my team. Suddenly the walls opened up. I was able to see where the bottlenecks were – and it became clear that one of my team had taken on far too many projects and tasks. As a result, she was struggling, and so was the entire practice.

Interestingly it wasn't long after that, that this member of my team ended up in hospital. This coincided with me getting married, preparing for a conference the following weekend and desperately trying to finish a book that was due for the conference.

Having Asana in place meant that I was set up to bring in help right away. I contacted a VA agency and found a VA who was able to come in and jump straight into my practice. She helped me free up the bottlenecks and get my practice back into flow at a time when I really needed it. And the reason that she was able to jump right in was because my practice was set up in Asana.

People often tell me that 'it's easy' for me – that being productive and organised is just something that I do well (and in contrast, they don't do well). But that's really not true at all. Just like many speakers and consultants, I'm a creator at heart. I am very organised, but that's because I put world-class organisational techniques and tools into place – including and especially Asana – so that I can do the things that I want to do in my practice.

This book represents what I've learned about harnessing the power of Asana in a consulting practice. It comes from my own experience but also the experience of helping many other consultants develop their own practices. It represents my experience with failed project management systems (and witnessing this in others' practices) and bringing Asana online for myself and many, many others.

This book doesn't lay out all the details of setting up an Asana account or give you a 'how-to guide' on using the basic functionality. One of the things that I love the most about Asana is that it's very easy to get across all these more basic elements – Asana offers loads of information and tutorials themselves and many VAs are trained in these processes. Additionally, there are many Asana experts who can help should you need further assistance.

This book is for speakers, experts and other consultants who are ready to elevate and grow their practices. It's designed to show you how to adopt and optimise Asana to meet those unique needs. It gives you the top steps to take and provides a mindset framework for creating an efficient and task-oriented team that can support you to achieve your practice goals.

This isn't a long book – or complicated. It's simple and to the point, and that's because simple is best! What this book will give you is some insight into the benefits of Asana for consultants, including speakers, thought leaders and experts, and some expert tips on how to use it to its best for your consulting practice.

I wrote this book because Asana changed my practice and gave me a way to proactively grow while building better team collaboration. I hope it helps you do the same. And if you have any other questions, just reach out. I'd love to help!

~ Jane

CHAPTER 1

The Critical Role of Project Management in Consulting

'A goal without a plan is just a wish.'

— **Antoine de Saint-Exupéry**

Time is money. This is true of all businesses, but especially in consultancy. For consultants, like speakers, thought leaders and experts, every minute of your time has value. And you likely know precisely what that is.

Because of this, it's absolutely vital that you understand where your time is being spent and how to make sure that your resources are being used strategically to further your business. You need to be able to optimise *all* your resources –

and that includes your time and energy – to ensure that you're progressing in line with your commitments and goals.

High-performing project management is the way to go.

The benefits of a project management system

I have a client who's an expert in her field, and a few years ago, her practice was gaining a lot of traction. She was getting really busy meeting with clients, delivering projects, speaking and more. But the busier she got, the more often she woke up at night, panicking about what she wasn't remembering.

Her task and project management system consisted of a notebook, calendars, lists and even notifications on her phone. This worked OK while her practice was small. But as she got bigger and more in demand, deadlines slipped by, and things started getting missed. She needed a high-performance project management system to get her back on track and keep her there.

Project management isn't just a way to track what is or is not done. Instead, as one of my clients says, 'It's like having another team member in your practice.' This 'person' (or system) is the custodian of everything that happens, has happened and is meant to happen in your practice. It's the one nagging you about what needs to be done – or better, nagging your team about what needs to be done – scheduling tasks, creating projects, managing your workflow and keeping you on track. It simply remembers all the things so that you don't need to.

This is important for all businesses. But it's uniquely important for consultants. That's because consultants face a unique business challenge. Unlike internal hires who are onboarded, given a transition period and expected to build up to their full potential, consultants are expected to simply hit the ground running. They're brought on for a limited amount of time and often at a high price point. So clients expect them to deliver high-impact results on budget and on time, every time.

These are high pressures that consultants may feel on top of the typical pressures of running a practice. So while project management is important for all businesses, it can truly make or break a consultant's growing practice.

So what are the benefits of a high-performing project management system?

- **Frees up your time and focus.** When your time is freed up from running the more mundane or everyday tasks of your practice, you're able to focus on the higher-value activities. Instead of spending time on administrative responsibilities, scheduling or emailing, you can spend your time on client development and delivering on your core expertise.

- **Enhances your client service.** Project management systems give you more visibility into workflows, responsibilities and deadlines so that your team is better able to meet all project deadlines and deliver excellent results for your clients.

- **Meets your business goals.** These systems allow your team to work more collaboratively and efficiently, which supports the achievement of your business goals overall. They'll have more access to information, an improved framework for meeting daily tasks and requirements and more ability to collaborate across all the areas of your practice.

- **Saves you money.** Having a system that does the hard work for you frees up your staff for business growth and revenue-raising activities. This saves you money in the long run.

Why Asana?

It's likely that as a consultant, you're already very clear on the importance of a high-performance project management system. But what should you choose? There are many options out there that you could use, systems such as Monday, Click Up, Insightly and more. But for my consulting clients, I always recommend Asana.

In fact, I believe Asana is the ideal tool for consulting businesses. I use it myself in my own consulting practice and have personally seen all the amazing benefits of having this 'person' on my team.

Asana outperforms other project management systems for a huge number of reasons, not the least of which is that it's very easy to use, has an intuitive user interface (that is easy for your team to interact with) and offers a huge range of features. It also has a free option that, unlike other systems, supports unlimited teams, projects, messaging, activity logs, file storage, multiple project views and more. It even integrates with time-tracking tools. For many people, especially if you only ever have 15 users and only need to manage basic projects, the free plan works very well.

Benefits of Asana

So what are some of the benefits of Asana specifically?

- **Multiple project views.** With Asana, you can view projects and manage tasks in several different ways, including timelines, calendars, lists, portfolios and workloads. That means that each team member can manage their tasks and projects in the way that works best for them, and you get visibility in a way that works best for you.

- **Team collaboration.** Asana can act as a single point of truth for your team collaboration. Through this system, you can share documents, communicate one-on-one and as a group, comment on projects and tasks, assign tasks and workflows between team members and more. The calendar view lets teams plan around each other's schedules and, importantly, around yours. This is particularly useful if you have a geographically dispersed team, as most consultants do.

- **Integration.** Asana integrates with over 100 third-party apps. This includes email apps, messaging tools, and file and communication tools. For example, Slack, Dropbox, Google Drive, Zoom, Salesforce and Zapier all integrate well with Asana.

- **Automation.** Asana gives you the ability to automate repetitive tasks and processes. So rather than having to manually set recurring tasks each time (for example), which will eat into your or your team's time and energy, automating means you only need to do it once. This saves you time and money and frees you up to do more value-adding work.

- **User-friendly layout.** Asana's dashboard is user-friendly and easy for new team members to pick up. If you have specific features that are important to your practice, you can customise the dashboard to best suit your needs.

- **Efficiency of scale.** One of the best things about Asana is the efficiency of scale. Because it's well-known, well used and well-regarded, a lot of help is available. There are tutorials from Asana themselves, as well as loads of information from other experts out there in the form of YouTube videos, how-to blogs and more. There are also many Asana Certified Pros – like myself – who are able to jump in and help you and your team get up and running.

At the end of the day, having a high-performance task and project management system brings many, many benefits to your practice. I became an Asana Certified Pro to help my clients better set up their practices with Asana. But I've also seen an incredible difference in my own team and my own practice.

What the research says

Asana delivers real results. Data from a study[1] of interviewed Asana customers with 5,564 employees using an average of 146 business applications and representing a diverse global cross-section including the US, Japan, Australia, Czechia, France, Germany, Singapore, the Middle East, Africa and Europe, shows us that Asana users have:

437% 3-year ROI	70% more time for creative/ innovative work	42% faster To execute business processes
34% less time Spent on admin tasks	33% less time Spent on emails	55% less time Searching for information
11% higher Client satisfaction	34% more Projects delivered on time	72% higher employee satisfaction
13% faster Completion of projects	42% faster Execution of business processes	40% more Business processed completed

The business value of collaboration grows when you and your team are able to work together collaboratively and effectively and when your work is tied to outcomes. Asana helps you do that. In fact, the IDC research group valued the higher

---

1   IDC Research Inc. (2021). *The Business Value of Asana*. [White paper]. Available at https://asana.com/resources/idc-business-value-of-asana.

employee productivity delivered by Asana at an average of nearly $3,500 USD per year per employee[2].

---

2   IDC. *The Business Value of Asana.*

In our own consulting practices

Using Asana, and using it well, has allowed me to really optimise all the benefits of a fantastic project management system for my own practice. It's allowed me to benefit from having another incredible team member on my side. I've seen it do the same for so many of my own consulting clients, and it can do the same for you.

There is power in increased visibility, collaboration and communication, optimised workflows and timely project delivery. Yes, there are monetary benefits, but it will also bring you peace and confidence that the day-to-day requirements of your practice are being met. You'll be able to focus on the big picture, and, like my client, you won't have to worry about waking up in a panic worrying that you've missed something.

Of course, if you're reading this and thinking of all the reasons why a project management system isn't right for you right now, read on. We'll discuss some of the things that might be holding you back from embracing any project management system and why taking the plunge could make the difference between thriving and dying in the consulting world.

CHAPTER 2

What Holds Us Back From Making the Change and Why We Should Get Over It

'Lost time is never found again.'

– Benjamin Franklin

Asana can help save you time, energy and even resources. It can help you keep your team on task, your projects on deadline, and your clients happy. But even when we understand all the benefits of a new system, we might struggle to implement it. And we might also find it difficult to get buy-in from our team members.

Why is that? What holds us and our team back from embracing a high-performance project management system that we know will benefit our clients and our practice overall?

What holds us back?

So what are some of the things that hold us back from making the switch to Asana?

Fear of change

Getting started with any new tool or system is often the most difficult part of the entire implementation process. This is particularly true if you have a team in place who are used to, and comfortable with, the status quo. While you might see the benefits of the new system – in this case, Asana – your team may see it as more work.

Additionally, there are many people who simply fear change. This can be particularly true in the work setting where your team may feel that by changing their daily processes, you are somehow devaluing the work they've done to date or making some kind of commentary on their capabilities.

Switching to Asana, particularly if you've been relying on a patched together suite of tools or apps to run your practice previously, could be a big shift for your team. But simply reassure them that the end goal is to create more space to focus on client work and bring more ease and flow to their own work and your practice overall. And be sure to let them know that they will be given the time and training required to adapt to the new system. For your own reassurance, know that Asana is one of the best and easiest systems to onboard.

Fear of 'wasting' resources

Often what holds my clients back is the worry that they won't be able to manage the ongoing costs of new technology, including Asana, and that a new tool will just turn out to be another waste of money. I know this feeling well having gone through a number of project management tools (and wasting a lot of time and money!) before finding Asana.

The good news with Asana is that the barrier to entry is extremely low. Often the free option is more than enough. In fact, I don't even recommend getting a paid subscription until you have quite a few team members, and you're ready to focus on the growth of your business.

When you are ready to level up, Asana is very reasonable in cost, especially at the lowest tier. And the value that you get from Asana far outweighs the cost. In fact, I've heard from clients and experienced myself how having this system can be like having another person – a very organised and efficient person – in your business. So for a very low fee you have an organisational expert on hand. In that case, it's easy to see it for the value that it really does offer.

Fear of losing time

It's true that adopting any new technology or tool will likely slow you and your team down for the short term. Learning how to work in Asana – like any new piece of software – and use it to your best advantage, just takes time. Often this can feel frustrating to your team, who see that their old way of doing things is faster in the beginning. It may lead them to dig their heels in, and keep using the old system, which they already know and feel comfortable with.

However, one of the benefits to getting Asana up and running is creating clear processes that will ultimately save everyone time in the long run. But it's not just about saving time on the front end. The transparency, collaboration and clarity that Asana can bring stops mistakes and miscommunications that could be even more costly to fix. So even when the technology is taking more time in the beginning, it's likely already saving your team time in the long run.

Inability to take action

Sometimes we're held back simply by our inability to take action. This could be for a number of reasons, but by far the most common for speakers, experts and thought leaders is busy-ness.

Often when our practices are growing and we're getting busier and busier, we find ourselves stuck in the daily race to just keep up. We don't feel that we have time (or energy) to focus on streamlining our processes because we're struggling just to keep our heads above water. Because of that, we choose to do nothing. Or, really, we choose to only focus on putting out the fires. And that leaves us feeling that we can't make any real changes.

But this is actually the time that we should be making changes – that we should be adopting new systems, like Asana, that can help us see our way out of the overwhelm and into a more streamlined and productive system. When you choose to do nothing, then you're actually choosing to do nothing to move towards your big goals. But if you choose to proactively take action, then you'll find yourself moving towards your goals and bigger and better success in the future.

Fear of technical complexity

Like anything new, the fear that it's simply going to be too technical for you or your team to manage is one thing that often holds us back from adopting any new system, including a performance management system. Of course, adjusting to anything new will require some learning, and Asana is no different. And the ability to take up this new software will depend on the tech savviness of yourself and your team, as well as the amount of time and energy you put into training.

It may feel that it's simply too hard and that your team, particularly if they've been using less digital-heavy systems to date, just won't be able to cope with the new technology. This is different from the fear of lost time or pushback from the team. This is more around the idea that they simply won't be able to use Asana to its full potential and leave you in the same position you're currently in and your new tool languishing with disuse.

Asana, however, is quite an intuitive system. And, unlike other management systems, it is highly supported by training provided free by Asana themselves. Moreover, because it's a popular system, there's help to be had locally as well.

Of all the individuals and practices that I've worked with to onboard Asana, all have easily implemented it from a technical standpoint.

Why it's worth it

At the end of the day, getting over your fears of new tech, a new system or time or money lost, and just finding the time to implement any new system is worth it. This is demonstrated by the Optimise Model below.

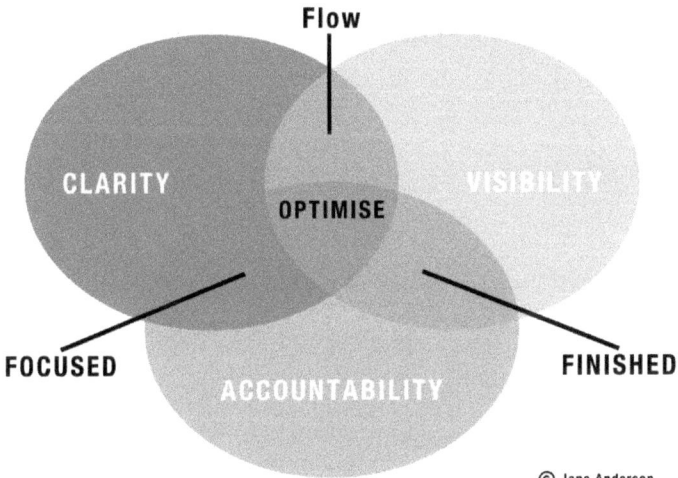

Flow

CLARITY · **VISIBILITY**

OPTIMISE

FOCUSED · **ACCOUNTABILITY** · **FINISHED**

© Jane Anderson

Optimise Model

Unpacking the Optimise Model

The Optimise Model lays out the benefits of embracing Asana as a consultant, whether you're a thought leader, an expert or a speaker, including greater clarity, more visibility, higher accountability and, ultimately, the ability to optimise your business. Let's explore this further.

Clarity

As consultants, it's sometimes a bit difficult to have clear goals, responsibilities and task definitions that set the objectives and expectations for each project that we need to deliver. A lot of that is because we have such a wide variety of projects to manage as consultants. This could (and probably does) include our keynotes, delivery to our multitude of different clients and managing the projects needed to grow our business generally. Too much of what we do lies within ourselves – our own thought expertise, speaking ability, and expert delivery.

Getting a team on board to manage all these diverse requirements is vital. But when we do diversify the responsibilities, as we should, we lose clarity on who is doing what and when. And when we lose clarity, we lose our ability to track our progress and ensure our goals are being met.

Asana gives us this clarity back. It allows us to outline tasks clearly, set deadlines and describe deliverables that align with our goals. It also allows us to track progress and ensure that the desired outcomes are met in the timeframes we want. We can even see the percentage of progress that's being made on each project and by each person. And when we have this clarity back, we'll have conquered the first step needed to optimise our consulting business.

Visibility

One of the challenges we have as consultants with a team supporting our work is the ability to see what is going on and when. Many of my consulting clients, and myself included, have struggled with seeing into our business, but visibility is crucial to monitor workflow, track progress against deadlines and anticipate (and beat!) potential bottlenecks.

Asana creates a space where we can really dig into our business and 'see' where we are. We can see the status of tasks, the progress being made and the due dates, of course. But more importantly, we can see how everyone in our business is performing and where they may have too many tasks assigned or have capacity to take on more tasks. This releases those bottlenecks that slow down our practice generally and supports better project management overall.

Accountability

The final element highlights the importance of creating space for team members to be accountable for their tasks. As consultants, we often work with a variety of clients and organisations, and as speakers, we deliver to a wide variety of audiences at a wide variety of conferences and events. Having accountability among your team will help you maintain a high standard of work and ensure that everyone is utilised on the tasks and projects that suit them and your practice best.

Asana helps us accomplish this by allowing us to assign tasks to specific individuals, set deadlines and goals, see the number and types of tasks assigned to each member of the team and follow up on task completion. Each of these promotes accountability. Even better, they promote *self-accountability*. So rather than you having to follow up on every task, Asana follows up for you, allowing your team to see where they need to focus their efforts and attention.

At the intersections

Where the circles overlap within the model, they form combinations that show how Asana delivers additional benefits.

Clarity + Visibility

When clarity and visibility overlap, it creates an environment where it's easier to be in flow. A flow state is described as being 'that sense of fluidity between your body and mind, where you are totally absorbed by and deeply focused on something, beyond the point of distraction'[1]. And when you're in this space, you're able to work efficiently and effectively, as can your team.

Clarity + Accountability

Where clarity and accountability overlap, you get a more focused team and a more focused approach to work generally. Here you have clear expectations and self-accountability that

---

1   Headspace. 'What is a flow state and what are its benefits?' Available at https://www.headspace.com/articles/flow-state#:~:text=You%20 may%20have%20experienced%20a,Your%20senses%20are%20 heightened.

leads to greater responsibility with individual team members and a more directed and efficient effort overall.

Visibility + Accountability

Where visibility and accountability overlap, you get a project that is 'finished'. In other words, you get a space where team members are accountable, and project progress is visible, and, therefore, the project is more likely to be finished successfully. In this space, you'll find that tasks are completed and goals are met.

Optimise

Finally, in the centre of the model, you get a practice (and a team) that is entirely 'optimised'. This is where your workflow, resources and team members are all working at their optimal levels, in flow, with focus and with a goal of taking projects into the finished space.

When you're here, everything isn't always perfect, but you're in a position to see exactly where everyone and everything is in your practice. And when things don't go right (and they won't always go right!), you and your individual team members can quickly identify what's working well and what isn't and make adjustments to improve efficiency and effectiveness.

The Optimise Model emphasises the importance of having a structured approach to managing consulting projects. With Asana, you get the vital elements – clear communication, visibility and individual responsibility – which can help you elevate your consulting business to exceptional.

Your Next Steps

There are many reasons that we might initially struggle to give Asana the green light – some we might feel ourselves, and some we might get from our team. But there's no other system that can give us so much clarity, visibility and accountability in our practices and help us to ultimately optimise it for better efficiency and better results in the long run. It's worth it!

But now that we know how much value Asana can bring to our practices, we'll also want to know how to best bring it in to get the most out of it. As consultants, there are some specific things we can do. So, let's find out the top five ways to optimise Asana for your consulting practice.

CHAPTER 3

5 Ways to Optimise Asana for Your Consulting Practice

'Time is really the only capital that any human has, and the only thing he can't afford to lose.'

– Albert Einstein

Albert Einstein made this profound statement long before any modern project management system was even dreamed of. Yet, it's highly applicable to our modern organisational methods. And it's particularly true in the dynamic and demanding consulting world.

As consultants, the meticulous organisation of tasks, the delegation of responsibilities and the efficient use of time are hugely important to our success, not to mention, our sanity.

While I'm a huge proponent of Asana for nearly everyone, this chapter is all about how to really get the most out of it if you're a consultant, speaker or expert. These top five suggestions will help you use Asana to its best and optimise your time and resources, to make sure that you're able to stay focused on your core competencies and deliver value to your clients.

5 ways to optimise Asana in your consulting practice

1. Assign to your team, not to yourself

The most important thing that you should be doing in your consulting practice is staying OUT of Asana. And by that, I mean you should not be assigning tasks to yourself. While you can certainly (and should absolutely) be using Asana to see what's happening in your practice and to ensure that you're progressing towards your practice goals, you should not have any tasks assigned directly to you.

This doesn't mean that you won't have tasks that you need to do yourself. But anything that you need to be doing and that will take up your time should be managed in Asana by your VA or EA, who will then put those items into your calendar. You will then only be looking at your calendar to understand where you need to spend your time, rather than having to work out of the project management system.

This is important for you as a consultant because it will help your team to prioritise and triage your work while ensuring that they are the ones that are accountable for making sure that it happens. What that means is that the important work that you need to be doing gets done, while still leaving you free to spend your mental energy on your clients,

In effect, staying *out* of Asana allows you to stay *in* your genius. It reduces the amount of time that you need to spend managing other people by helping them self-manage and enabling them to manage you better. You can think of this as getting the monkey off your back. It lifts the weight, allowing you to get as much off your own mind as possible.

A study conducted by Stanford University and cited in the *BBC* found that 35% of CEOs felt that their delegation skills needed improvement, and 37% said that they were already trying to improve these skills.[1] What this shows is that people – even incredibly high achievers – are far too likely to remain sitting in the minutiae of their business rather than expanding their own genius. They simply struggle to let go.

As Richard Branson said, 'If you really want to grow as an entrepreneur, you've got to learn to delegate.' And Asana is the ultimate delegation tool.

---

1   Borzykowski, B. 'Why you can't delegate — and how to fix.' 2 April 2015. *BBC*. Available at ithttps://www.bbc.com/worklife/article/20150401-why-you-find-it-hard-to-delegate#:~:text=A%20 2013%20executive%20coaching%20survey,it's%20been%20 difficult%20to%20learn.

I was working with a client, Peter, who struggled with delegating in his own practice. When he came to me, he was finding it challenging to keep on top of all the project requirements that needed to be done. In trying to figure out what was going wrong in his practice, we did an audit on his Asana processes. It turned out that 50% of the tasks in his practice were assigned to his VA, but almost 50% of the tasks were assigned to him.

Once we realised this, I immediately started to reassign these tasks. As those tasks went from his responsibility to his team's responsibility, he stopped having to manage his own practice, schedule and time. This freed him up to do the things that he was best at, and his practice flourished.

Like with Peter, the most important thing you can do as a consultant in your practice management is to stay out of Asana. Check on your tasks and make sure that your VA is not assigning anything to you. If they have, assign it back to them and explain why that's happening. The tasks that you need to do should then be placed in your calendar by your VA. At the end of the day, the delegation will allow your business to flourish as well!

2. Map your practice activities

The second step to ensuring that Asana is working best for you as a consultant is to take the time to map your practice activities across all your platforms, including Asana. Having a visual architectural map of your practice will give you immense clarity when it comes to your filing systems and the best ways to structure workflows. If you don't have this, you and your team will waste an incredible amount of time looking for things, determining the next task to tackle and simply managing the day-to-day fires in your practice. This will create drag and friction and introduce mistakes and errors into your practice overall.

On the other hand, having a practice map is like having a blueprint of the ideal design of your practice. You and your team will know where to find things quickly and easily and will be able to see how the tasks can be accomplished most effectively in your practice.

Of course, this is easier said than done. In his book *The Personal Efficiency Program: How to Stop Feeling Overwhelmed and Win Back Control of Your Work!*, Kerry Glesson undertook informal research that found that estimated around 90% of people have never actually been shown how to work at a desk. In other words, they've never been shown how to operate and use filing systems and workflows effectively, despite these being core processes in every business and practice.

This has an impact on the effectiveness of teams today. In fact, research shows us that the average person spends six weeks per year trying to find things (that's an hour and a half per day).[2] Executives are wasting six weeks per year searching for important documents as well.[3] And much of this will be due to simply not having these skills.

You just have to calculate the cost of that lost time to see how this could negatively impact your practice. For example, if you have a local VA who's charging you $50 an hour, then six weeks of their time costs you $12,000. Even if you have an offshore VA that you're paying $15 an hour, that's still $3,600 a year. And, of course, there's your own cost of lost time, which can be huge. If you're charging your time out at $1,000 per hour, and you're spending six weeks of your year trying to find things, that's $240,000 a year it's costing you wasted time.

Having a blueprint and a map of your practice will support a strong filing structure and the workflow of your practice

---

2   'Productivity Stats: The Cost of Lost Productivity, Poor Time Management, Inability to Prioritize, and Procrastination'. A Clear Path. Available at https://aclearpath.net/productivity-stats/.
3   'Productivity Stats. A Clear Path.

overall. And that means you will save money in the long run too.

Steps for mapping your practices

1. The first step to creating your practice map is to write out all the aspects of your practice. This includes identifying the processes that need to be done in your practice, clearly defining them and stating what you will gain from that process.

2. As your second step you will need to capture who, what, when, where and how each task in that process will occur. In this step, you should also speak to your team members and other stakeholders to ensure that you have correctly captured the work that they're doing, as well as to help you uncover any inefficiencies and find the best way of doing things.

3. The third step in your practice mapping is to align everything with your filing and project workflows within Asana. This will allow you to streamline your processes to make sure that you and your team are working at your most efficient. This will

also mean that you'll be in a much better position to scale your practice more quickly.

As Albert Einstein said, 'You can't use an old map to explore a new world.' Aligning Asana closely with your new practice map will help you grow into the future.

3. Weekly status updates

Since, as the genius in your consulting space, you won't be in Asana every day, you should be having weekly meetings to get status updates. This will allow you to take control of the week ahead and reduce any nasty surprises.

During these scheduled reviews, you'll want to ensure that every task has an assignee and a due date and check that tasks are on track by commenting on each one. When you don't have regular updates – and this really means weekly – then mistakes can occur. You'll miss tasks, or deadlines will slip by, and the accumulation of this over time creates a lot of pressure, friction and stress within your business and for yourself.

David Allen, author of *Getting Things Done: The Art of Stress-Free Productivity*, also stressed the need to review all your projects in as much detail as you need to at least once a week. He says, 'If you do, your systems will work. If you don't, your systems won't work.'

Honestly, it's as simple as that. I've seen this for myself. I worked with a lovely client by the name of Sandra, who used Asana in her practice. One of the tasks that needed to be done was sending a particular article to a client via post. However, because she wasn't doing her weekly status updates, she didn't notice that this task hadn't been assigned to someone and didn't have a due date.

The result was that the task was missed, and the client didn't get the parcel. And because Sandra wasn't doing her weekly updates, she missed that it was missed. The client was very upset, and Sandra had to scramble to remedy the situation.

This entire error could have been avoided if she'd just had a weekly status update and gone through each project, double-checking that each task had an assignee and a due date. If she'd had this review process in place, the task would have been picked up, and she would have been able to give her client the kind of service she expected.

When you and your team have these weekly updates, you won't be waking up at 3am in a panic, wondering what happened to certain tasks or projects. You'll know that you have the system in place that will prevent things from falling through the cracks and will keep your practice moving forward.

Steps for creating weekly status updates

4. Ask your VA to block 30 to 45 minutes once a week to go through the projects. Our team does this on a Friday afternoon because things are a bit quieter at the end of the week, and this sets us up for the upcoming week.

5. During your weekly updates, make sure that you're checking that tasks are assigned and due dates are implemented. You'll also want to confirm that important tasks are being managed for the week ahead.

4. Setting and tracking goals

In Asana, goals tracking is available in the premium versions (that's Advanced and Enterprise tiers). While I don't always recommend premium versions when you're just starting out, when you do have a team supporting your consulting practice, it's well worth considering since this will give you access to really valuable additional functionality, including Asana's goals feature.

Goals tracking connects your work with your purpose. It helps you to keep your practice and teams aligned, agile and focused on achieving milestones on their projects. It also connects to portfolios (another feature in the premium versions) which can give you even deeper insights into the functioning of your practice.

Having goals in your practice is like having a north star that guides you and helps you keep on the right track. It's easy for you and your team to get caught up in the world of minutiae, ticking off tasks each day. But each person needs to see the direct connection between what they do every day and how it contributes to the overall purpose within the practice.

By using goals in Asana, you can connect each task to a project and each project to a goal and each goal to your overall mission. Of course, to do this well you must have KPIs set out for each project and for each team member. For example, it might be one team member's responsibility to make sure the newsletter goes out each week. Set that goal clearly in Asana, and ensure that's a KPI for that achievement.

Connecting each task, project and goal (including personal KPIs) is vital to the efficient functioning of your practice. If you don't have this connection, you and your team are likely to end up with a breakdown between the understanding of why we're here and what we're actually doing each day.

Brian Tracy, speaker and self-development expert, once said, 'A goal without a plan is only a dream'. Jess Pryce-Jones, who wrote the book, *Happiness at Work: Maximizing Your Psychological Capital for Success*, works with organisations to identify people's sense of happiness and engagement at work. In her research, she's found that the number one reason why people feel engaged and happy at work is their sense of contribution. At the end of the day, that contribution comes from an alignment between the tasks they're doing and the specific goal and mission of the organisation.

Steps for setting and tracking goals

1. First, decide on the three biggest goals for your practice for the year.
2. Second, decide on the three goals for each quarter.
3. Third, break down each goal and connect it to your projects.
4. Fourth, assign the responsibility for each goal to a team member.

5. Create insightful reporting

When you first start keeping track of all the tasks for your team, it's easy to end up in the weeds. This can happen because you just start focusing on the tasks that need to be done as opposed to really checking on the capacity of your team. The best way to ensure your team is operating at their most efficient is to ask, are they heading in the right direction? Are they coping? Are they overwhelmed? Are they being underutilised? And how can you best optimise the team that you have?

Asana gives you that data through insightful reporting. Again, this is available in the premium versions, but when you're running a practice with a team, then getting these kinds of insights can really help progress.

As the expert, you need a higher level of reporting to check that projects are on track and that your team is working to their capacity. If you don't, then your team can very easily become overwhelmed. While this can happen at any time, when you're receiving insightful reporting, you can catch it quickly and redirect them.

Alternatively, reporting helps you to identify which projects might need more attention and support. You'll be better able to see when it's time to bring on a new team member or to outsource some tasks so that your internal team can focus more on what they need to do.

Peter Drucker said, 'You can't manage what you don't measure, and if you're not measuring, and reporting, and keeping an eye on what's going on, you'll end up with bottlenecks really quickly.'

I had a situation once, which I mentioned briefly in the introduction to this book, where I had hired both a local Australian online business manager and an offshore VA. The VA was hired to help take the pressure off my OBM and leave her with more time to focus on big-picture projects. The VA would then take on the more detailed, technical, everyday tasks.

The challenge was that my OBM was reluctant to let go of a lot of tasks. She wanted to keep control of the practice by keeping control of the tasks. Her fear was that things weren't going to get done properly. But what it actually meant was that the VA wasn't able to do her job, and I was paying her to do not much at all. Most importantly, everything was constantly delayed.

This situation went on for a while without me understanding why it was happening. But once I started using Asana, and had access to the reporting tool, I could then see the bottlenecks in my practice. Suddenly I had visibility and awareness, and that meant that I could do something about them. Finally I was able to unblock the bottlenecks and get a more efficient team and practice.

When it comes to your practice, if you haven't got visibility and awareness, you really can't do anything. The beauty and the challenge with a system like Asana is that no one can hide. Everything is visible. You can see everything. It's all transparent. And it means that you can get on top of things quickly if things aren't going well.

With Asana's reporting, I would recommend that you use these three key reports and insights:

1. **Overdue tasks.** The overdue tasks report is really simple but invaluable. You can see what is outstanding very quickly and can tell if someone is struggling. When you see that a team member is overcapacity, you can take steps to reduce their load or give them any other support they might need.

2. **Projects per assignee.** This report keeps track of the number of projects that each of your team members has assigned to them. This allows you to see who has the bandwidth to take on more or help out other team members.

Of course, different tasks take different amounts of time and different areas of expertise. So if you are running a practice that's generating, say, $500,000 or more, then you might have a VA or EA to help support you. You probably don't want people in these roles to have as much on their plate with their projects because they need more reactivity – that is, they need to be able to respond quickly to you and your clients and have time to manage your calendar and emails. So they might have 20 to 25 projects.

On the other hand, you might have 50 projects for your program manager, which would include all the individual clients that you're coaching, the elements of the program that you're delivering and all the tasks related to delivering a keynote. With the projects per assignee report, you can then look at the number of tasks per assignee that are coming up in the next week, and this will give you an idea of how much each of your team has on their plate, and you can see if you need to deploy any more resources to help, or if they have the capacity to take on more generally.

3. **Portfolios.** The portfolio tool is available in the premium version as well. And using this tool to organise your projects allows you to see a holistic

view of your practice. When you view your projects through the portfolio management view, then you're able to monitor their health and progress in real-time, keep your team updated on the next steps and get more data for analysis. The portfolio progress section also gives an in-depth snapshot of the status of any portfolio that you and your team might be working on.

Conclusion

Asana is about more than just managing tasks. It's about managing your practice with the acumen of a seasoned strategist and the insight of an industry expert. Asana becomes your partner in your pocket, delivering insights, helping you meet your goals and tracking your goals each day.

Asana can be transformative for any business, but it can truly revolutionise your consulting practice when you optimise it well. Using Asana demonstrates your commitment to excellence, and through it, you can lead your practice into a symphony of organised effort, strategic focus and dynamic team building.

It has worked for me, and it's worked for many of my clients. Let's hear from a couple of them in the next chapter.

CHAPTER 4

Case Studies

'Productivity is being able to do things that you were never able to do before.'

– Franz Kafka

The consultancy world is fast-paced and always changing. And in order to grow and respond in the consulting industry you need efficient collaboration and strong project management in your practice.

Asana has helped many of my clients achieve incredible growth. In this chapter, I want to showcase some real consultants who have had amazing success implementing Asana into their practices.

As we navigate through these stories, You'll see unique insights into how this robust project management tool can help manage a transformative shift in how your projects are delivered and your practice goals met. And you'll gain a deeper understanding of how Asana can be tailored to meet the dynamic needs of your consulting practice and your team.

Jane Bedggood – Principal, Jane's Virtual Solutions Pty Ltd

Jane is a highly experienced EA/VA for expert thought leaders. Through her own virtual solutions consulting practice, she helps other consultants, including speakers and educators, to manage and grow their own practices as well.

For Jane, one of the biggest challenges is being able to come into another consultant's business and get up to speed quickly and efficiently. To make a real impact, she needs to be able to get into the minds of her clients fast so that she can really dive into the nitty gritty of their practice. Of course, this involves task orientation but also a mindset of trying to stay one step ahead so that she can bring a proactive approach to working in her client's businesses.

Working with a wide variety of clients, Jane also needs to be highly flexible. Some of her clients run large public events and deliver multi-day conference keynotes and as such have large databases to manage. Other of her clients have more internal practices that include in-house programs and coaching. Each of these has different kinds of processes and procedures. Jane needs to be totally organised and able to delve into each of these types of practices (and more) with a single project management system.

That's why she came to our team for Practice in a Box. Practice in a Box helps consultants set up an entire practice's tasks, procedures and projects in a single day. And a major part of this is setting up Asana.

Practice in a Box, but in particular Asana, has been a game-changer for Jane. She loves Asana for its organisation, saying that once it's set up, 'you can't forget anything', and for its flexibility, which can be tweaked for each client's unique practice (including her own). She appreciates that she can use the list format and simply tick off tasks as they're completed or use it as a board, which helps her to visualise the progress of projects. Most importantly, it allows her to dive into her clients' businesses, tackling day-to-day tasks while providing visibility and collaboration with their internal teams and her own team.

Jane says, 'It's all there for everybody to see what everyone is doing. Each task can be assigned and has a set due date, so nothing is forgotten.'

She continues, 'This is important when I'm running practices for a few different people, especially when I have a new client coming on board. It's important to have Asana set up so that it really suits that unique practice.'

'When all those things are in place, the practice just works. All the tasks are in place. The templates are set up and can easily be updated so they're suitable for the new client. And everything is running smoothly.'

Jane knows that this not only improves the practice of her clients but it also improves her own mental bandwidth, capacity and creativity. Rather than using her mental space (and a notebook), she's moved all this to Asana, taking it out of the notebook and out of her head and leaving it to her digital team member (Asana).

She says, 'It's made a huge difference. Huge difference. Because there's so much clarity and it's so collaborative, it takes away the need for loads of meetings, calls and emails. It actually gives more time back to me, the client and the whole team. And Asana has helped my clients have a gangbuster year – in fact, their best year ever.'

'It's also enabled me to start thinking proactively. For one client, I'm able to do some research, reach out to people and even start prepping for her sales meetings.'

She says, 'It's like having another employee in my business.'

Jane sees Asana as a project manager. It has the capacity to think of all the things. And now that her practice is set up correctly, it's like a running treadmill, and all Jane has to do is jump on it. She's been able to help her clients with book launches, keynote presentations, preparing proposals and onboarding new team members while also reducing meetings, increasing clarity and boosting transparency.

Jane has a new client coming on board now, and she's in the midst of setting him up on Asana as well. She says, 'I'll just show him how it works, and then we'll tweak it together so that both of us are across the different steps. It will increase our capacity to accomplish his tasks and projects!'

Meldrick Advincula – EA to Dr Louise Mahler

Meldrick Advincula, known as MC, works as the EA to Dr Louise Mahler, one of the busiest experts and keynote speakers currently working in the consulting industry. As an offshore EA (he resides in the Philippines), he really understands the value of Asana in bridging the distance and allowing him to work *in* Louise's practice, despite being physically distant.

Working with such a busy consultant, with programs, retreats, speaking engagements, conference gigs and a coaching practice, means that MC has a lot on his plate, including managing her calendar and bookings, organising meetings and calls, reaching out to clients, answering inquiries, putting on events, arranging travel and dealing with speaking bureaus, among others. What that means is that MC must be flexible. He needs to be able to stay on top of Louise's varied practice requirements while also agilely pivoting to deal with the different needs of her practice each day.

He says, 'Every day I need to be able to say, "Whatever task you throw at me, I'm ready!"'

He acknowledges that when he first stepped into Louise's business, it was very challenging because they didn't have a good system in place. He says, 'The absence of a system made it challenging for me to keep track of all the tasks, deadlines and project details. I needed to deal with different projects all the time, as well as reports and seeing results. Communicating was also a challenge because we only used chats, like through Slack. That made it difficult to attach files and really put processes in place for workflows.'

Getting Louise onboarded onto Asana has helped MC and Louise's practice immensely. It's allowed him to stay on top of the varied tasks and projects that he needs to manage while also creating flow and ease in the practice generally.

He says, 'Since we've implemented Asana, it's really helped me to know each task and what to do every day. Communication has become much easier, as well as determining the steps and processes needed for each specific project. It's also helped with time management because when I'm dealing with different tasks each day, the system will let me know what I need to focus on during my workday so that I can prioritise those tasks.

And if unexpected things crop up, I can look at the priorities and understand at a glance what can wait until tomorrow. So I can focus on what I've got to deal with to handle the current problem.'

Asana has allowed MC to build a customised practice management system for Louise. It embraces centralised management, so he can create, assign and track all tasks in one place, which streamlines the workflow for himself and Louise's other team members.

For example, when it comes to managing Louise's speaking gigs, MC can now easily ensure that the plan is organised, the confirmation goes out, the conference organiser receives Louise's bio and introduction and that her speaking video has been done, among all the other things that need to be accomplished to ensure her keynote goes smoothly. He's also very easily able to manage the onboarding process for Louise's coaching clients, including sending them her books, establishing the workflows for delivery of the coaching program and being able to see Louise's capacity overall. In other words, he can run all her projects, keynotes and coaching clients from a single platform.

MC says, 'It would be a nightmare running all this without Asana. My brain would be all over the place, and I'd constantly be running to check my notes and worrying that something was going to be forgotten. But because it's all in Asana, all the projects for speaking, coaching, micro-events, retreats and public workshops, then it takes me one minute to do tasks that might otherwise take me an hour. I just use the templates, set the due dates and get started. It's very easy for me to set up because it's all in one place.'

The ease that MC experiences working in Louise's business extends beyond just project management. It actually helps MC with the decision-making process. With Asana in place, MC feels empowered to make decisions very quickly and handle inquiries and client contacts when Louise is busy travelling, speaking or delivering. MC can ensure everything is in place for Louise's various responsibilities, so all Louise has to do is turn up to the pre-event call (for example) and debrief with the client.

This keeps Louise in her expertise rather than in the details of managing her practice. And it gives MC the ability to be efficient and proactive in managing her practice instead. While Louise has an eagle-eyed view of what is going on, MC is down in the details and together (with Asana in the supporting role), they make the perfect pair.

MC sums up the value of Asana by saying, 'Louise sleeps very well at night. She knows that we have the system. She knows that we're on track on all her projects, and that's a big thing for a speaker, coach and expert because she can just stay in her expertise. It's all about trust. And because of Asana, Louise can trust that everything is being taken care of and can support her and her practice.'

Conclusion

Diving into how Asana has changed the game for consultants like Jane and MC shows us that it isn't just about managing tasks. It's about transformation. Asana is a powerhouse. It helps VAs, EAs, speakers, experts, thought leaders and all consultants to organise their practice *and* see real growth.

These case studies highlight how crucial a solid project management tool is in the consultancy world. It makes it easier to adapt, react, collaborate, communicate and stay ahead. It's clear that Asana isn't just another tool. It's like having another (experienced and detail-oriented) team member in your practice. And this will elevate every aspect of your consulting business.

Conclusion

When you run a consulting practice, you have unique needs for task and project management. But as we've seen, Asana is an excellent way to meet all those needs. Once you have it set up and optimised, you'll be able to sleep well at night knowing that things won't be missed and that your practice won't be swamped by inefficiencies, miscommunications and missed opportunities.

Adopting Asana will allow you to transform your business and reshape your consulting practice taking it from disarray to harmony. This is evident in my practice and in MC's and Jane's (and their consultants!), as well as in the practices of the many other consultants that I've worked with to adopt Asana.

It's a paradigm shift, a mindset reset, that moves you out of your systems and out of overwhelm, allowing your team to step in and manage your processes. This allows you to stay in your expertise and accomplish so much more now and in the future.

My hope is that this book has helped you to see the incredible benefits that Asana can offer you as a consultant, as well as the things that will help you take it to the next level for your consultancy practice. You'll be able to stay out of the details of Asana while still getting the high-level insights that will let you drive the strategy and focus on your practice. By mapping and understanding all the parts of your practice, you'll be confident that everything is being done that needs to be done.

Asana can lift your consultancy game, bringing ease and flow into your speaking gigs and other expert and thought leader activities. It can truly change your practice!

Let's make the change!

If you haven't yet gotten started with Asana, there is lots of information available on how to do that, both from Asana's own platform and from other experts in the industry. This book isn't designed to deliver all the information you need to implement Asana step by step. Instead, the concepts, ideas and suggestions in this book are designed to help you elevate your practice by utilising Asana in a way that's uniquely optimised for consultants.

Of course, you have a unique practice as well. And Asana can be used to develop the templates, workflows and processes that are specific to you. At the end of the day, you'll be able to create an efficient and task-oriented team that can support you to achieve your practice goals.

I would love to hear about your experiences implementing Asana into your consultancy practice and the outcomes that you experience. Please get in touch with me at jane@jane-anderson.com.au to share! And if you do need help – either implementing Asana – or taking additional steps to align Asana with your needs, get in touch with our team. We'd love to help!

Jane

Work With Jane

In a world of constant change, there is a greater need for consultants and experts in their fields to lead and help their clients navigate change. To do this, they need a highly influential personal brand, catalyst content and effective business support to build their tribe.

With over 25 years of experience and being named one of the top three branding experts in the world, Jane has helped over 180,000 people build their identity and influence. She is a certified speaker and coach and has been featured on *Sky Business*, *The Today Show*, *The Age*, *Sydney Morning Herald*, *BBC* and *Management Today*.

The author of 12 books, Jane typically speaks at conferences, runs workshops, consults and coaches. She also has a particular focus on female leaders, helping them to build their personal brands, thought leadership and sales.

Jane holds one of the top 1% viewed LinkedIn profiles and is the host of the *Jane Anderson Show* podcast where she has interviewed modern thinkers such as Seth Godin.

She has also won over 50 branding, marketing, business and coaching industry awards.

CORPORATE CLIENTS HAVE INCLUDED:

Telstra, International Rice Research Institute, Wesfarmers, Amadeus, Virgin Australia, IKEA, LEGO, Mercedes-Benz, Australian Medical Association, Shell Energy and Workcover.

Book a time to chat here:

https://calendly.com/jane-0877/complimentary-discussion or contact Jane's team at support@jane-anderson.com.au or

+61 7 3841 7772.

Alternatively, jump on Jane's website at www.jane-anderson.com.au to learn about her workshops, speaking and coaching programs.

Other Titles By Jane Anderson

Nurture

Exceptionality

Women with Influence

Put Yourself Out There

Catalyst Content

Personal Power Planner

Expert to Influencer

Connect

Trusted

Impact

Confidence